THE ENCYCLOPEDIA OF PSYCHOACTIVE DRUGS

TREATING MENTAL ILLNESS

THE ENCYCLOPEDIA OF PSYCHOACTIVE DRUGS

TREATING MENTAL ILLNESS

ROBERT BYCK, M.D.
Yale University School of Medicine

GENERAL EDITOR (U.S.A.)
Professor Solomon H. Snyder, M.D.
*Distinguished Service Professor of Neuroscience, Pharmacology
and Psychiatry at
The Johns Hopkins University School of Medicine*

GENERAL EDITOR (U.K.)
Professor Malcolm H. Lader, D.Sc., Ph.D., M.D., F.R.C. Psych.
*Professor of Clinical Psychopharmacology
at the Institute of Psychiatry, University of London,
and Honorary Consultant to the Bethlem Royal and Maudsley
Hospitals*

Burke Publishing Company Limited
LONDON   TORONTO   NEW YORK

First published in the United States of America 1986
© 1986 by Chelsea House Publishers,
a division of Chelsea House Educational Communications, Inc.
This edition first published 1988
New material contained in this edition
© Burke Publishing Company Limited 1988

Acknowledgements
The publishers are grateful to those individuals and organizations, including St
Bartholomews Hospital, for permission given to use material and illustrations
included in this publication.

CIP data
Byck, Robert.
  Treating Mental Illness
  1. Man. Mental disorders. Drug therapy
  I. Title.   II. Series
  616.89'18
  ISBN 0 222 01467 9 Hardbound
  ISBN 0 222 01468 7 Paperback

Burke Publishing Company Limited
Pegasus House, 116-120 Golden Lane, London EC1Y 0TL, England.
Printed in Spain by Jerez Industrial, S.A.

CONTENTS

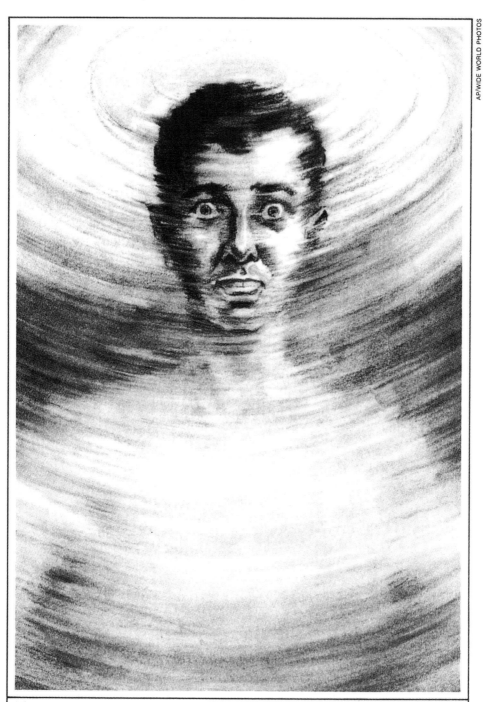

This drawing dramatically captures the feelings of dreadful anxiety and frantic confusion that beset many mental patients as they try to survive in a world that they do not understand.

INTRODUCTION

The late twentieth century has seen the rapid growth of both the legitimate medical use and the illicit, non-medical abuse of an increasing number of drugs which affect the mind. Both use and abuse are very high in general in the United States of America and great concern is voiced there. Other Western countries are not far behind and cannot afford to ignore the matter or to shrug off the consequent problems. Nevertheless, differences between countries may be marked and significant: they reflect such factors as social habits, economic status, attitude towards the young and towards drugs and the ways in which health care is provided and laws are enacted and enforced.

Drug abuse particularly concerns the young but other age groups are not immune. Alcoholism in middle-aged men and increasingly in middle-aged women is one example, tranquillizers in women another. Even the old may become alcoholic or dependent on their barbiturates. And the most widespread form of addiction, and the one with the most dire consequences to health, is cigarette-smoking.

Why do so many drug problems start in the teenage and even pre-teenage years? These years are critical in the human life-cycle as they involve maturation from child to adult. During these relatively few years, adolescents face the difficult task of equipping themselves physically and intellectually for adulthood and of establishing goals that make adult life worthwhile while coping with the search for personal identity, assuming their sexual roles and learning to come to terms with authority. During this intense period of growth

Extraction de la Pierre de Folie *by Hieronymus Bosch shows a "surgeon" removing the "stone of madness" from a patient's head. Throughout history societies have invented remedies, some successful, some not, for insanity.*

and activity, bewilderment and conflict are inevitable, and peer pressure to experiment and to escape from life's apparent problems becomes overwhelming. Drugs are increasingly available and offer a tempting,respite.

Unfortunately, the consequences may be serious. But the penalties for drug-taking must be put into perspective. Thus, addicts die from heroin addiction but people also die from alcoholism and even more from smoking-related diseases. Also, one must separate the direct effects of drug-taking from those indirectly related to the life-style of so many addicts. The problems of most addicts include many factors other than drug-taking itself. The chaotic existence or social deterioration of some may be the cause rather than the effect of drug abuse.

Drug use and abuse must be set into its social context. It reflects a complex interaction between the drug substance (naturally-occurring or synthetic), the person (psychologically normal or abnormal), and society (vigorous or sick). Fads affect drug-taking, as with most other human activities, with drugs being heavily abused one year and unfashionable the next. Such swings also typify society's response to drug abuse. Opiates were readily available in European pharmacies in the last century but are stringently controlled now. Marijuana is accepted and alcohol forbidden in many Islamic countries; the reverse obtains in most Western countries.

The use of psychoactive drugs dates back to prehistory. Opium was used in Ancient Egypt to alleviate pain and its main constituent, morphine, remains a favoured drug for pain relief. Alcohol was incorporated into religious ceremonies in the cradles of civilization in the Near and Middle East and has been a focus of social activity ever since. Coca leaf has been chewed by the Andean Indians to lessen fatigue; and its modern derivative, cocaine, was used as a local anaesthetic. More recently, a succession of psychoactive drugs have been synthesized, developed and introduced into medicine to allay psychological distress and to treat psychiatric illness. But, even so, these innovations may present unexpected problems, such as the difficulties in stopping the long-term use of tranquillizers or slimming-pills, even when taken under medical supervision.

The Encyclopedia of Psychoactive Drugs provides infor-

A 17th-century engraving of moonstruck (lunatic) women dancing in the street. Insanity has inspired fear throughout the ages. Only in the 20th century have we begun to deal with mental illness in an enlightened way.

mation about the nature of the effects on mind and body of alcohol and drugs and the possible results of abuse. Topics include where the drugs come from, how they are made, how they affect the body and how the body deals with these chemicals; the effects on the mind, thinking, emotions, the will and the intellect are detailed; the processes of use and abuse are discussed, as are the consequences for everyday activities such as school work, employment, driving and dealing with other people. Pointers to identifying drug users and to ways of helping them are provided. In particular, this series aims to dispel myths about drug-taking and to present the facts as objectively as possible without all the emotional distortion and obscurity which surrounds the subject. We seek neither to exaggerate nor to play down the complex topics concerning various forms of drug abuse. We hope that young people will find answers to their questions and that others—parents and teachers, for example—will also find the series helpful.

The series was originally written for American readers by American experts. Often the problem with a drug is particularly pressing in the USA or even largely confined to that country. We have invited a series of British experts to adapt the series for use in non-American English-speaking countries and believe that this widening of scope has successfully increased the relevance of these books to take account of the international drug scene.

This volume does not in itself deal directly with drugs of abuse. Rather, it outlines three main classes of medicines used to treat psychiatric conditions, namely the antipsychotics, the antidepressants and the mood-stabilizing agents. These drugs have greatly altered both the practice and the theory of psychiatry.

Written by Dr Robert Byck, an American psychiatrist and adapted by Professor Malcolm Lader for readers outside the USA, the text provides a non-technical account of the main psychiatric conditions and the important drugs used to treat them.

M. H. Lader

A collage entitled Minds in Torment *serves to illustrate the state of a person suffering from mental illness. Many emotional disorders are physiologically based and can be treated by prescribed psychiatric drugs,.*

CHAPTER 1

AN OVERVIEW

Research into the chemistry of the brain has revealed the physiological basis of many types of mental illness. With this knowledge scientists have been able to develop specific drugs to treat a wide range of emotional disturbances. Although many of these drugs are powerful and mood altering, they rarely produce any therapeutic effect on so-called "normal" people. Furthermore, unlike illegal drugs, psychiatric drugs are rarely if ever abused. This book will discuss these drugs, focusing on how they work, when they are beneficial, and the type of patients for whom they provide help.

Mental Health Professionals

Mental disorders are treated by a number of different kinds of professionals. Although only medical doctors can prescribe and administer psychiatric drugs, a brief description of the various types of people who work with the mentally disturbed will provide a helpful overall picture of the mental health field.

A *psychiatrist* is a medical doctor who has also taken some years of training in the treatment of mental disease. Psychiatrists are trained to distinguish between the symptoms of physical disease and the symptoms associated with psychological disorders. Their training usually enables them to practice individual, family and group psychotherapy. Because they are doctors, they can legally prescribe drugs.

A *psychotherapist* is an individual trained to use one of the many forms of "talking therapy" that have been developed from various theories on how to treat psychological disorders. Rather than using drugs to treat mental disorders, a psychotherapist relies on discussion techniques that help patients examine their feelings about themselves and their lives. A psychotherapist may also have various other professional qualifications, such as a graduate degree in social work.

A *psychoanalyst* is a professional trained and certified to practice psychoanalysis, a method used to reveal to patients psychological conflicts that they are unaware of. Usually, but not always, the psychoanalyst is a doctor trained in psychiatry. Psychoanalysis is a form of treatment developed from the theories of the Austrian psychiatrist Sigmund Freud (1856–1939). Psychoanalysts believe that mental illness often is caused by the repression of painful past experiences. They

Sigmund Freud, the father of psychoanalysis. According to Freudian theory, mental illness is often caused by a person's attempt to repress painful past experiences.

THE BETTMANN ARCHIVE

feel that by bringing forgotten memories to the surface, the sources of psychological conflicts can be located. If the patients are made aware of these conflicts, the psychological disorders can be diminished or eliminated.

This type of therapy may involve treatment four or five times a week. During these sessions the psychoanalyst employs specific and clearly defined techniques that help patients recall forgotten and repressed experiences and relate them to their current behaviour. Although psychoanalysts rarely prescribe drugs, they are legally entitled to do so if they are also doctors.

A *psychologist* is a person who usually has an advanced degree, often a Ph.D., in clinical psychology. He or she practises many kinds of psychotherapy, including behaviour therapy, a technique that uses rewards and punishments to change the way people act. Many psychologists are well trained in the diagnosis of mental illness. Few, however, are experienced in recognizing the differences between physical illness and mental disease. Because they do not have medical degrees they are not allowed to prescibe drugs.

Historical Background of Psychiatric Drugs

In the middle of the 19th century the French doctor Moreau de Tours noted the remarkable similarity between some of the symptoms associated with mental disease and the psychological state caused by the use of hashish, a drug made from the *Cannabis sativa* plant. His book *Hashish and Mental Illness* was one of the first works to suggest that mental disorders might be caused by chemical imbalances in the body rather than by environmental or psychological factors. More than a century later scientists are still debating the extent and importance of these biochemical (the chemical reactions in living organisms) factors. Many researchers now believe that the root causes of most mental disturbances are associated with chemical changes in the central nervous system (the system in the body that includes the brain and spinal cord and that coordinates physical activity). Whatever the cause may be, one fact is now certain. It is possible to reduce the symptoms of many psychiatric illnesses with drugs that affect the central nervous system.

Many of the drugs now being used in the treatment of mental disorders were first developed in the 1950s. Modern *psychopharmacology,* or the study of the effects of drugs on the mind, is frequently traced to Albert Hofmann's discovery of LSD in the late 1940s. Nevertheless, the notion that *mental* illness is similar to *medical* illness can be traced to the 19th century, when some scientists proposed anatomical and chemical imbalances as the cause of mental disorders.

A revolution in the treatment of mental illness occurred in the early 1950s. Henri Laborit, a French surgeon was researching ways to prevent complications that occurred after surgery. He combined antihistaminic drugs (drugs that oppose the action of histamines, chemicals found in all body tissues and particularly associated with inflammation and allergic reactions) with other drugs given to patients prior to surgery. One of these antihistamines, promethazine, produced a state described as "euphoric quietude", a calm feeling of well-being.

In 1951 a new drug, 4560 RP, also known as chlorpromazine, was sent to Laborit, who experimented with the drug as a preventative against surgical shock and as a way to speed up anaesthesia. Laborit noticed that 4560 RP produced sleepiness and what he called "uninterestedness" (lack of interest in the environment) in patients. Although some psychiatrists had used 4560 RP in combination with other drugs in sleep therapy, Laborit was the first doctor to describe the drug's unique effects in reducing anxiety and agitation. He encouraged psychiatrists to administer it to patients.

Unlike all previous forms of treatment for psychosis, chlorpromazine seemed to have a long-term, dramatic effect on many different types of mental disorders. Its discovery ushered in a new era in psychiatry. News about the success of this revolutionary drug in treating mental illness spread quickly, and within five years it was being widely prescribed in French mental hospitals. Researchers reported that the drug was most effective in reducing the symptoms of psychosis when administered continuously for several weeks. Scientists began synthesizing and testing other similar compounds, until a wide range of drugs soon existed for the treatment of psychosis.

In 1949 an Austrian psychiatrist, John Cade, discovered that lithium salts could successfully treat the manic stage of manic-depressive psychosis (This disease is characterized by abrupt alternations of depression and mania, or frantic elation). However, it would be almost 20 years before lithium was accepted into psychiatric practice.

From India in the 1950s came another breakthrough— the discovery of a drug called *reserpine.* This drug was extracted from the root of *Rauwolfia serpentina,* or snake-root, a plant that had been used as a folk remedy for insanity for hundreds of years. The term *tranquillizer* was first used

A pharmacist prepares a drug in an apothecary shop in the 1800s. Hashish and Mental Illness, *a book by the 19th-century French doctor J.J. Moreau de Tours, was one of the first works to suggest that mental illness might be caused by chemical imbalances in the body. It has since been proved that the symptoms of some psychiatric illnesses can be alleviated by using drugs that affect the central nervous system.*

THE BETTMANN ARCHIVE

to describe the calming and mood stabilizing effects of reserpine, which was used to treat psychosis.

Drugs for Mental Illness

Pharmacologists and doctors divide drugs into three categories. Over-the-counter drugs, the most familiar, are usually readily available to the general public at pharmacies, supermarkets and grocery stores. Prescription drugs can be obtained only with a doctor's prescription. And lastly, there is a varied group of drugs that are used in self-treatment. They are often dangerous and sometimes illegal.

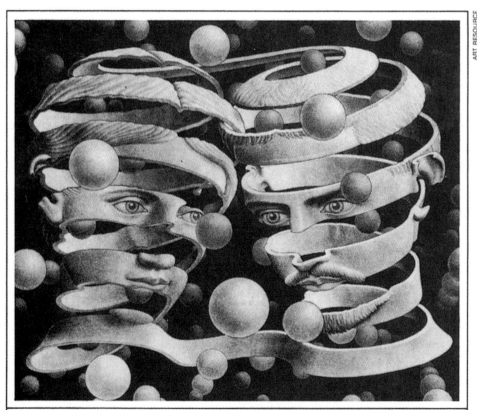

ART RESOURCE

Bond of Union, *a painting by the well-known Dutch contemporary artist Maurits Cornelis Escher, articulates the complex relationship between patient and therapist. Two of the basic requirements for successful psychoanalytic treatment are honesty and trust.*

Over-the-counter-drugs, or OTCs, include a large group of preparations of varying effectiveness. They include such medicines as ointments, cough medicines and aspirin. Once they have been tested and approved by the appropriate licensing authority in each country, OTCs are considered safe enough to be taken in the recommended doses without the advice of a doctor. OTCs are of no use in the treatment of psychiatric illness.

Prescription drugs are available only with a doctor's prescription. Possession of these drugs by anyone other than the person for whom the prescription was written is technically illegal. Prescription drugs are usually quite safe if used as directed. However, if the wrong dosage is taken or the wrong drug is prescibed for a particular illness, these drugs are potentially very dangerous.

Certain prescription drugs fall under the dangerous drugs legislation, and are "scheduled", meaning it is likely they may be abused and are therefore controlled. For example, heroin is a drug which is tightly controlled because it has no accepted medical use and has a high potential for abuse. Amphetamine is less tightly controlled because it has some accepted medical use and not just a potential for abuse. Though all of the drugs discussed in this volume are prescription drugs, none of them are scheduled. This means that the drugs used for the treatment of psychiatric illnesses neither lead to addiction nor produce pleasurable effects in "normal" individuals.

Self-medication often includes the use of drugs to regulate mood. These drugs may be commonly available substances, such as nicotine, alcohol and caffeine, or illegal drugs such as heroin, marijuana and cocaine. People often use drugs to try to treat the symptoms of their mental illness. Those who suffer from depression or anxiety may, for example, take sleeping pills or *antianxiety* (tension reducing) drugs. Others turn to heroin, cocaine, or amphetamines, in the mistaken belief that these illegal drugs can relieve their depression. In fact, "self-medication" is often the beginning of serious drug abuse problems. Such substances may be not only addictive but also physically and psychologically destructive. The long-term use of these drugs can only lead the user into serious drug abuse, thus compounding the very problems the sufferer was trying to treat.

Drug Names

Like all prescription drugs, each *psychotherapeutic* (a drug used for treating psychiatric illness) has several names. For example, 2,chlorophenothiazine is the chemical name of the drug more commonly referred to in medical usage by its generic name, chlorpromazine. In addition, drug manufacturers give their products trade names. In France and the UK chlorpromazine was given the trade name Largactil. When it was introduced into the United States, the American drug manufacturer chose the trade name Thorazine.

The gifted actress Frances Farmer, who achieved both celebrity and notoriety during the late 1930s and early 1940s, was subject to uncontrollable fits of violence and rage. She was eventually given a lobotomy, an action that many people feel was both inhumane and medically unjustifiable.

SPRINGER/BETTMANN FILM ARCHIVE

Drugs are also given group names, which indicate their effects or therapeutic purposes. For example, chlorpromazine and other similar drugs were catergorized in France as neuroleptic drugs. Today they are often called *antipsychotic drugs,* a term more descriptive of the use to which they are put. In this book we will discuss *antipsychotic drugs* (medications used to relieve mental disturbances), as well as *antidepressant drugs* (medications used to relieve depression) and *mood-stabilizing drugs*. These terms, although useful, are not necessarily fully descriptive. We can also refer to many of the antipsychotic drugs as *antihistaminic drugs,* thereby describing them according to their pharmacological action rather than by their therapeutic purpose. This class could also be called *dopamine-blocking drugs*. Here we are using as a descriptive term a specific effect that those drugs

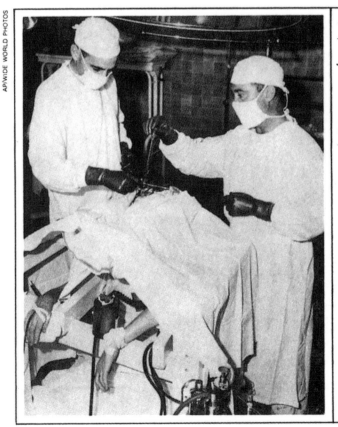

AP/WIDE WORLD PHOTOS

Neurosurgeons perform a pre-frontal lobotomy, which is a form of brain surgery used by some doctors to treat people suffering from violent and seemingly incurable forms of psychosis.

have on *dopamine* (a neurotransmitter, or a chemical present in the body that conveys signals between nerves).

Another way to name drugs is by their chemical group. For example, chlorpromazine is a *phenothiazine,* the name of the basic chemical that was modified to synthesize chlorpromazine. Drugs can also be classified by their chemical structure. One group of antidepressants is called *tricyclic* antidepressants, because the drugs in this particular group have three rings of carbon atoms in each molecule.

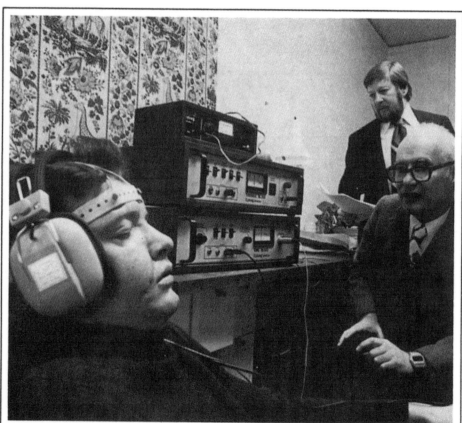

Scientists study sleep patterns of a patient they have taught to doze off naturally, without the aid of sleeping pills. Sleep therapy for psychiatric illness had its origins in the mid-19th century.

Drugs and Their Effects

Psychopharmacology, a specialized area within the field of pharmacology, is the study of the origin, properties, and effects of drugs that alter emotions and behaviour. Scientists working in the area of pharmacology have discovered some general principles that hold true for all drugs. Before we examine the drugs used to treat mental illness we need briefly to review these principles.

The specific chemical reactions produced by drugs in the body are quite complicated and irrelevant to our discussion. However, knowing the structure of a drug that

A tablet press used in the production of aspirin. Like the psychotherapeutic drugs, aspirin does not cure a disease, but rather decreases or alleviates the symptoms.

has therapeutic, or beneficial, effects can serve as a guide for chemists who hope to synthesize a new drug with similar actions. Unfortunately, most new drugs have been discovered accidentally.

One general principle of pharmacology is that the dose of a drug is directly related to the drug's effects. The higher the dose, the greater the effects. Unfortunately, this also holds true for side effects (undesirable effects of the drug). The effectiveness of a treatment is therefore frequently limited by the side effects that may occur. However, sensitivity to the various effects of any given drug differs from patient to patient. One person may react to a particular drug with such severe trembling or shaking that use of the drug must be discontinued. Somebody else may be better able to tolerate the symptoms. When prescribing a drug, a doctor must take

The aftereffects of a heroin dose. Heroin, which is a physically addictive and highly dangerous narcotic, is sometimes seen as a last resort by individuals seeking escape from their problems through mindless oblivion.

into account not only the type of drug and its potency, but also the individual patient.

For a drug to be effective in treating mental illness it must affect the brain, where the disturbance is located. Most psychotherapeutic drugs, however, also affect other organs besides the brain. It is frequently those effects that are noticed first by the patient. Patients taking psychotherapeutic drugs must have an open relationship with their doctor so that they can feel free to discuss any suspicions or anxieties about side effects. The doctor may, for example, be able to adjust the dosage or the drug-taking schedule so that the patient suffers less from the side effects. Some of these undesirable side effects can be treated with other drugs.

Most of us are familiar with the effects of alcohol and aspirin. We can learn a few things about all drugs by thinking about the characteristics of alcohol and aspirin and how they relate to psychotherapeutic drugs. Alcohol is a drug that acts on the brain and changes the functioning of mental processes. Because it is quickly absorbed through the stomach into the blood, we feel alcohol's effects almost immediately. Some of the side effects, such as nausea and stomach irritation, can be local (confined to a specific part of the body). Once the alcohol is absorbed, we begin to experience the mental effects, while the liver starts to detoxify the alcohol, or chemically change it to an inactive substance that is excreted, or eliminated, by the kidneys. Although all drugs go through the same processes of being absorbed and excreted by the body, not all drugs are detoxified. Some are still for the most part unchanged when they are excreted by the kidneys.

Unlike alcohol, most psychotherapeutic drugs stay in the body for a long period of time. Because they have what is known as a long duration of action, psychotherapeutic drugs can be taken in the evening and continue to have beneficial effects throughout the next day. As with alcohol and most other drugs, the effects of psychotherapeutic drugs will intensify and sometimes change as the dosage is increased.

Aspirin, like the psychotherapeutic drugs, cannot cure a disease, but rather decreases or removes the symptoms. Taken in recommended doses by a healthy person, aspirin will have no obvious effect on the brain. Most psychotherapeutic drugs, however, do affect "normal" people, but the immediate effects of these drugs are usually their side effects, not the desired effects. The higher the dose, the stronger the effect. Many of these drugs cause sleepiness and interfere with activities that require concentration, such as driving.

As we mentioned earlier, people have different levels of tolerance for the side effects of psychotherapeutic drugs. Some of these side effects can be lessened by the use of other drugs, but others are an apparently necessary cost of treatment. Drug treatment of psychiatric illness is a powerful and radical approach, and it should be used only when the possible benefits outweigh the possible risks.

Treating Mental Illness

The symptoms of mental illness may appear gradually and go unnoticed for some time. However, a person who has trouble functioning or maintaining personal relationships should certainly seek—or be encouraged to seek—professional help.

Someone who experiences a sudden onset of symptoms of mental illness should be seen immediately by a doctor. Such symptoms may be the result of drug use, of physical illness, or of a physical change in the brain, such as a tumour. Once the doctor has determined that the problem is a psychiatric illness—one related to disorders of thought, behaviour, and mood—the use of psychotherapeutic drugs in treating the disease may be considered. The severity and duration of the symptoms usually determine whether the disturbance is best treated with drugs. Many people who have become distressed with the events or patterns in their lives may require psychotherapy to work out the problems. Depending on the severity of the patient's symptoms, a doctor may recommend both psychotherapy and drugs.

Nancy: A Case Study

Nancy was a troubled 17-year-old student who, over the previous six months, had become secretive and isolated, frequently locking herself in her room. She took no interest in her physical appearance, and her performance at school deteriorated sharply. She constantly heard voices that she felt were controlling her life, telling her she was a bad person who should be punished. To calm herself, she began to smoke marijuana. Nancy had become decidedly paranoid, afraid that her family and friends were trying to harm her. Plagued by morbid fantasies about food and a fear that dead animals would poison her, Nancy refused to eat meat. She often used nonsensical words to express her thoughts.

When asked by a doctor to describe her feelings, Nancy said with no emotion: "I am dead, and you are all rotting.

A scene from the film **The Snake pit,** *which portrayed the horrible conditions of a mental asylum of the 1940s. This film focused attention on the need for improving conditions in psychiatric wards.*

Rottingham is meat. That's the place where we can meet".

Further investigation uncovered a history of mental illness in Nancy's family. Her paternal uncle, who suffered from recurrent nervous breakdowns, had been in and out of mental hospitals for years. Most significantly, it also became clear that the deterioration of Nancy's mental health began just after the sudden death of her father in a car accident.

A psychiatrist dealing with someone like Nancy must consider a number of possibilities. Perhaps her bizarre behaviour and anxieties were induced by the abuse of drugs. Then, too, a brain tumour could have been responsible for her symptoms. In addition, her current state may have been a temporary, yet extreme, sign of the grief and sense of loss she felt because of her father's death. People in mourning often have *hallucinations,* sensory impressions that have no basis in reality.

Quite obviously, Nancy's overall behaviour was markedly abnormal, but what exactly was the source of her problems? Many healthy young adults have tried drugs, have mental illness in their families, and have experienced the death of a close family member. What made Nancy different?

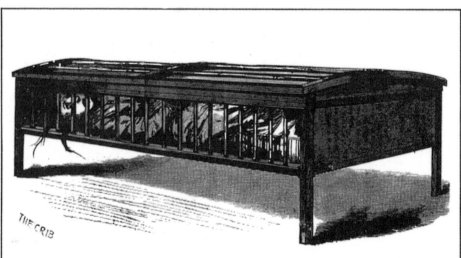

THE BETTMANN ARCHIVE

THE CRIB

An 1880 woodcut shows an object known as the "crib" which was used in the Victorian period to restrain unmanageable victims of insanity. A variety of other traditional forms of restraint included straitjackets and manacles.

A trained psychiatric professional could certainly conclude that Nancy had a *psychosis,* a condition in which a person's abilities to think, evaluate, communicate, remember, respond emotionally and behave appropriately are so impaired that he or she is unable to cope with the ordinary demands of life. Nancy's symptoms also fit the description of *schizophrenia,* a mental disorder characterized by a loss of contact with reality. Late adolescence is frequently the time when the symptoms of this disorder first become evident.

In cases like Nancy's, special tests such as brain scans and blood tests, which are designed to measure metabolic imbalances, are necessary. Her doctor would probably also want to test her urine to determine whether she was using drugs which might be causing or heightening her psychosis. Once all the medical data had been analyzed and Nancy had been extensively interviewed, a psychiatrist would be ready to decide on a course of treatment. Such treatment might well include an antipsychotic drug if she were diagnosed as suffering from acute schizophrenia.

In past centuries the cruel and inhuman treatment of madness, as shown in this 18th-century sketch, reflected society's superstitions and fears regarding insanity, which was commonly perceived as the work of the devil.

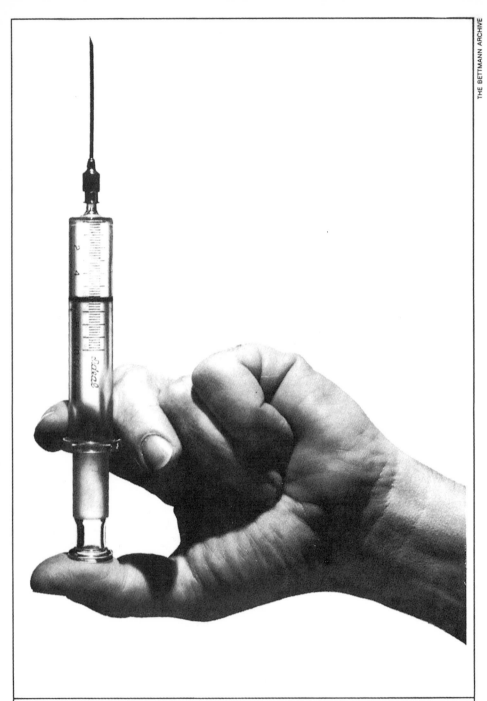

Drugs such as morphine can reach the brain quickly if taken through a hypodermic needle. Most antipsychotic drugs, however, are ingested orally and must be used for several weeks before they produce the desired effects.

CHAPTER 2

ANTIPSYCHOTIC DRUGS

*T*he original antipsychotic drugs all had chemical structures derived from phenothiazine. Researchers experimented
with many variations of the chemical structure of this
molecule to see whether they had benefits and side effects
similar to chlorpromazine.

The most striking similarity among the antipsychotic
drugs was that all such compounds were dopamine-blocking
drugs. As we mentioned earlier, dopamine is a neurotransmitter—a chemical substance found in the brain that
acts as a transmitter of messages between nerve cells.

Scientists originally relied on behavioural testing of rats
to screen chemicals for antipsychotic activity, but present
methods involve direct testing for dopamine-blocking activity in the brains of experimental animals. The discovery of
dopamine-blocking activity has led doctors to believe that
the onset of schizophrenia is related to an abnormality in the
dopamine transmission system in the brain.

Schizophrenia is the most common of the psychoses, and
affects approximately one percent of the population in all
countries where statistics have been gathered. Although
standards exist that define the disease, there is still some
concern that it may not be one disease but rather several
different diseases with common symptoms. Schizophrenia
may occur in late adolescence or early adulthood in two
apparently distinct forms. In one form, exemplified by Nancy
in our first case history, the patient grows up normally until
there is a fairly rapid degeneration of thought and behaviour.
In the other form, the patient is considered odd and asocial
(withdrawn) from early childhood, and acute psychosis

symptoms are superimposed on a long-standing withdrawn behaviour pattern.

Schizophrenics do not have "split" personalities, and are not "dumb". In fact, they may be very intelligent, but because of their mental illness they cannot function successfully in their work situation. In the past, schizophrenics have been repeatedly hospitalized for psychiatric treatment. Today, for medical, humanitarian and economic reasons, doctors and other psychiatric health care workers are trying to decrease the number and duration of hospital stays. One of the most impressive results of the drug treatment revolution in psychiatry has been the reduction of both the number of patients in mental hospitals and the average length of their stay.

Pharmacology

About 20 antipsychotic drugs are presently available in most countries. Although they differ in their potency, all can be equally effective in the treatment of psychoses. On the other hand, their side effects can be very different. To help explain the pharmacology of the antipsychotics, chlorpromazine can be used as a model.

Chlorpromazine comes in three forms—as pills or capsules, in a liquid state for oral use and in a liquid state for injections. How a drug is taken often determines how quickly it takes effect. Some drugs, such as chlorpromazine, are metabolized, or broken down, in the liver. When a drug is taken by mouth, it passes through the liver on its first trip through the bloodstream. When chlorpromazine is given by injection, however, much larger amounts may reach the brain before any metabolism occurs. An injected dose of chlorpromazine would therefore be smaller than a dose taken orally.

The first effect we often see in a patient taking chlorpromazine is sleepiness. All antipsychotic drugs have sedative, or tranquillizing, effects. Some drugs, such as chlorpromazine and thioridazine (Mellaril), are more likely than others to induce sedation in even the most anxious or agitated patients. In addition to its antipsychotic properties, chlorpromazine also helps to reduce nausea. When it is prescribed for this purpose to otherwise normal patients, its sedative property is seen as a side effect. Thus, whereas sedation is a therapeutic effect when chlorpromazine is used for treating psychiatric problems, it is a side effect when the drug is used to treat nausea.

In some patients with "organic brain syndrome", a psychotic condition caused by brain disease or tumours, chlorpromazine may decrease the thought disorder and agitation within a few hours. However, chlorpromazine and related drugs require repeated administration for weeks or months to produce their striking therapeutic changes in schizophrenic individuals.

Side Effects

Chlorpromazine and, to a certain extent, all other antipsychotic drugs block a portion of the *sympathetic nervous system,* which controls the constriction of the blood vessels (the

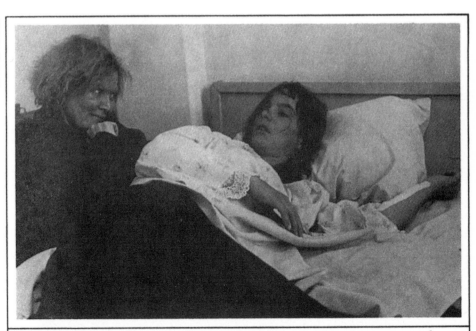

The 1977 film **I Never Promised You a Rose Garden** *was based upon Hannah Green's autobiography and depicted how the author was cured of teenage schizophrenia through her relationship with a skilled psychiatrist.*

sympathetic nervous system is part of the central nervous system, which controls involuntary bodily functions). These drugs are called *alpha adrenergic blocking agents,* meaning that they have properties that can prevent the proper flow of blood and oxygen to the brain. Thus, patients who take these drugs may feel faint or dizzy when they stand up too quickly.

Chlorpromazine, acting like *atropine,* a substance naturally present in the body, is also a blocker of the *parasympathetic nervous system* (this system controls involuntary activity such as sweating and contraction of the intestine). Patients taking chlorpromazine and other antipsychotics often suffer from a dry mouth and a decrease in perspiration. Older men, in particular, may experience difficulty with urination. Because of its resemblance to atropine, chlorpromazine is never given to patients who might have taken one

This painting, entitled Life Story, *was done by a schizophrenic patient with suicidal tendencies. Contrary to popular belief, many victims of schizophrenia are highly intelligent, but tend to see life as a collage of disassociated, and often frightening, impressions.*

of the hallucinogenic drugs that has atropine-like effects. It is also not given to patients whose psychosis has been caused by the use of PCP (phencyclidine, or angel dust, a dangerous drug that produces unpredictable effects, including stimulation, depression, and hallucinations). Some of the other antipsychotic drugs, such as fluphenazine, have less atropine-like effects.

Chlorpromazine and similar drugs also affect the body's hormone systems, partly as a result of the dopamine-blocking effect thought to produce the drug's therapeutic action. For example, non-nursing women who take chlorpromazine sometimes start to secrete milk. The production of milk is normally prevented by the presence of the *prolactin inhibiting factor,* probably the neurotransmitter dopamine. But because chlorpromazine has a dopamine-blocking effect,

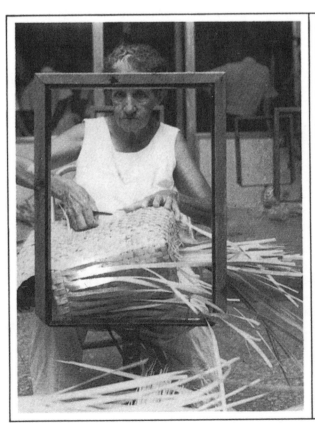

A patient weaves a basket at a psychiatric hospital in Cuba. Hospitals will often combine drug therapy with individual, family and group psychotherapy in order to help the patient cope with the outside world.

the prolactin is stimulated and the body begins to lactate, or produce milk. Although *galactorrhea,* or the excessive flow of milk, can be a very disturbing side effect, it can be treated with other drugs.

Many antipsychotic drugs also cause *photosensitivity,* a condition in which the skin reacts abnormally to light. Patients who use these drugs should therefore apply a powerful sunscreen lotion before they go outside. Patients must also be aware of the fact that these drugs intensify the effects of alcohol. This makes it very hazardous for individuals using antipsychotic drugs to drink and drive a car or operate potentially dangerous machinery.

Neurological Side Effects

The most striking side effect produced by chlorpromazine and other antipsychotic drugs is their influence on body control. Although these neurological reactions are common to all antipsychotic drugs, some medicines, such as thiorida-

ART RESOURCE

Blurred vision is one of the unpleasant side effects of antipsychotic drugs. Other side effects include dry mouth, increase or decrease in perspiration, dizziness and muscular weakness or rigidity.

zine, are less likely than others, such as haloperidol, to cause these effects.

One serious neurological side effect includes a group of symptoms that closely resembles those associated with Parkinson's disease, an ailment most common among older people. Although the actual cause of the disease remains a mystery, we do know that Parkinson's victims suffer a lack of dopamine in the nuclei of certain brain cells. Because the antipsychotics block dopamine, they produce Parkinson-like symptoms. These include fine tremors, a facial expression-lessness known as *Parkinson's mask* and muscular weakness and rigidity. The tremor occurs only at rest, not during sleep or intentional movement. People suffering from this disease may jerk when they try to move their arms or legs, and in severe cases they may feel painfully stiff and experience difficulty walking. Parkinsonism is treated with L-DOPA, a chemical that is converted into dopamine in the brain. In some cases it has produced considerable improvement.

Antipsychotic drugs also produce a condition called

The precise role that psychiatric drugs play in the treatment of psychosis has not yet been determined. Medical personnel are kept abreast of developments in the field of drug therapy by a variety of medical journals.

akathisia, the inability to sit still or maintain a resting posture. This side effect is confusing to both patient and doctor because the symptoms are frequently similar to the agitation caused by the patient's mental illness.

Occasionally, during the early stages of treatment with antipsychotics, a patient will have muscle spasms, often in the neck. Although this can be very frightening, this symptom can be treated successfully with an injection of certain drugs.

Tardive Dyskinesia

One additional neurological effect of antipsychotic-drug use, *tardive dyskinesia* (literally meaning "late-occurring difficulty with movement"), appears late in the treatment. In most cases, a drug's side effects occur during drug treatment and disappear when treatment is stopped. Tardive dyskinesia, however, first appears well into the course of treatment,

Cult leader Charles Manson was arrested and convicted of the brutal slaying of actress Sharon Tate and several of her associates in 1969. It is hoped that scientists can develop medication in the near future that can control the type of extreme psychosis that drove Manson and his "family" to commit such a horrible and senseless crime.

often when the dosage of the drug has been reduced. It appears most often in older people and is more likely to occur following the administration of large doses of an antipsychotic drug over a long period of time. Unfortunately, when the drug is suddenly discontinued, the tardive dyskinesia remains and may never go away. Tardive dyskinesia is the major reason that doctors are cautious about prescribing antipsychotic drugs, all of which have an equal probability of causing this disorder.

The most common form of tardive dyskinsia is characterized by involuntary mouth movements that resemble chewing, sometimes accompanied by an in-and-out move-

The feelings of helpless rage and entrapment sometimes experienced by victims of psychosis are powerfully evoked in this drawing by a schizophrenic mental patient. The discovery of antipsychotic drugs has revolutionized the treatment of schizophrenia.

ment of the tongue. More severe forms of this disorder include slow, rhythmic, automatic movements of the arms and torso, which can be both disconcerting and disfiguring. A person suffering from tardive dyskinesia has no control over these movements, and unfortunately there is no effective treatment.

Obviously, patients should be warned that this irreversible side effect may occur as a result of treatment. In general, true tardive dyskinesia occurs after at least three months of drug treatment, although many patients take the drugs for years with no sign of this disorder. Although tardive dyskinesia is disfiguring, it is rarely life threatening. Psychosis, however, can totally disrupt an individual's life. Patients with tardive dyskinesia often choose to continue taking antipsychotic medicine because they are unable to function without it. If an antipsychotic drug can successfully treat this serious illness, the benefit is worth the risk.

A therapy session at a hospital. Although "talk therapies" alone have questionable value in the treatment of psychosis, they are often a valuable supplement when used in conjunction with antipsychotic drugs.

Treating Side Effects with Drugs

The side effects caused by antipsychotic drugs are frequently treated with other drugs. The beneficial effects of antipsychotic drugs may not become apparent until weeks or even months after they are first taken, while most of their side effects occur almost immediately. Doctors therefore often find it necessary to minimize the negative effects by prescribing drugs that treat the side effects, so that patients will continue to take their medicine. After all, it does require an act of faith to take a medicine that may not produce its beneficial effects until months later.

Therapeutic Effects

The discovery of antipsychotic drugs has brought new hope to the treatment of schizophrenia. Successful drug treatment not only markedly decreases the patient's agitation and anxiety, but also relieves many of the major symptoms. Schizophrenics who have been treated for more than several weeks begin to think in a more organized manner. They reemerge from the private worlds they have created for themselves and start to establish contact with other people and with their surroundings. Patients who have undergone the new treatments appear more alive and active. They stop having delusions, and their hallucinations may completely disappear or persist in a much less disturbing form. The paranoia and feelings of being controlled by outside forces diminish. The treated patients gain a better sense of reality.

When manic, highly excited patients are treated with the antipsychotic drugs, their restlessness subsides, and their racing thoughts slow down. Since hostility often arises out of fear, the drugs' antianxiety properties often alleviate the manic patient's aggressiveness. (In contrast, the antianxiety or sedative properties of drugs like the barbiturates, benzodiazepines [antianxiety and sedative drugs, such as Valium], and alcohol often increase aggressiveness.) Without feeling as if they had been heavily sedated, patients begin to feel and act calmer. In addition, the antipsychotic drugs decrease the feelings of euphoric indifference, so that manic individuals once again begin to care about the consequences of their behaviour.

The antipsychotic drugs do not produce sudden drama-tic transformations, and not all of the changes occur in every patient. Sometimes a particular drug has little or no effect, making it necessary to try a different compound. Other times the dosage has to be adjusted to determine the optimal balance between therapeutic effects and side effects. Because of the nature of their illness, psychiatric patients are sometimes afraid that they are being poisoned and thus resist taking drugs. These feelings may be increased by the patient's understandable fear of the drug's side effects.

Because of the many problems associated with taking and administering antipsychotic drugs, the treatment of psychosis requires an all-out, comprehensive effort on the part of everyone involved with the patient. Although drugs vastly improve psychotic patients' perception of their environment, patients must be helped to learn how to relate positively to this often bewildering "new world". To meet these demands, today's mental hospitals often combine drug therapy with individual, family and group psychotherapy.

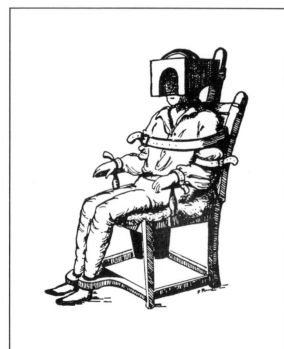

Before the discovery of antipsychotic drugs, such methods as this 18th-century "tranquillizing chair", which was designed by Dr Benjamin Rush, were used for the treatment of violent mental patients. A signatory of the Declaration of Independence, Rush was also an eminent doctor who wrote several books exploring the mysteries of mental disease.

THE BETTMANN ARCHIVE

Schizophrenic patients can never be entirely cured of their disease. For this reason, to supress the debilitating symptoms so that schizophrenics can function successfully outside an institution, long-term treatment with antipsychotic drugs may be required. In some cases, schizophrenic patients whose behaviour has been stabilized by drugs may experience intermittent psychotic episodes. In other cases, even with drug treatment, the behaviour of such patients may remain a bit strange. They are frequently unable to establish themselves socially and thus lead a marginal existence. Doctors must decide whether to keep the patient on a constant schedule of antipsychotic drugs or to administer them as the need arises. Because of the threat of tardive dyskinesia, doctors try to treat the mental illness by prescribing the smallest possible dosage to be taken intermittently.

Between episodes of their illness, manic-depressive people are frequently completely normal. The use of antipsychotic drugs to treat these patients is usually restricted to

An 1818 drawing of a circulating swing, which was used in attempts to bring patients out of deep depressions. Supposedly, the rotating and dizzying movements of the swing would somehow eliminate depression.

manic episodes, although chronic doses of lithium, a drug which we will discuss more fully, are often prescribed to prevent recurrences.

Other Treatments for Psychosis

Several forms of nondrug treatment have been both proposed and tried in order to help schizophrenic patients. Some radical theorists have proposed that instead of considering severely aberrant behaviour to be a symptom of mental illness, we should simply accept and tolerate as different the individuals who exhibit these symptoms. Most mental health professionals reject this theory, seeing it as being unhelpful and even destructive to patients.

Another approach calls for treating psychosis with large doses of vitamins. However, when scientifically tested and evaluated, this treatment did not prove to have any therapeutic benefits. On the other hand, this "megavitamin" treatment is not likely to be harmful, unless it deprives the patient of other effective treatment.

Psychotherapy has questionable value in the treatment

This 18th-century cartoon shows mental patients suffering from hallucinations. Such terrifying distortions of reality frequently haunt psychotic patients. The ability to relieve this type of illness is one of the great boons of modern pharmacology.

THE BETTMANN ARCHIVE

of acute psychosis. In fact, there is no evidence that it is any more effective than treatment with a *placebo* (a placebo is a harmless pill made of a substance that is either pharmacologically inert or active only in the treatment of unrelated symptoms). However, once the symptoms of psychosis have diminished, psychotherapy is successful in helping patients cope with the world.

Electroshock therapy (stimulating the brain with an electrical current to induce involuntary muscle contraction) is sometimes effective in treating agitated psychosis, but it is usually considered a measure of last resort. *Psychosurgery,* surgery performed on the brain, is rarely used today, although in certain cases it may be considered necessary.

The administration of antipsychotic drugs, often in conjunction with some form of psychotherapy, is now the most accepted form of treatment for psychosis. These treatments together make it possible for people who suffer from psychosis to function much more successfully in society.

UNITED ARTISTS

In the Academy Award-winning film One Flew Over the Cuckoo's Nest *(1975), Jack Nicholson (centre) portrays a man who feigns insanity to avoid prison. Unfortunately, the strategy backfires and he is forced to submit to such treatment as electroshock therapy and, finally, a pre-frontal lobotomy.*

Melancholia, *a work by the famous 16th-century German painter and engraver Albrecht Dürer, depicts the artist's symbolic view of depression, a condition that is characterized by feelings of despondency and sadness and has affected people throughout the ages.*

CHAPTER 3

DEPRESSION

Depression is not an easy concept to define. The word is used to describe a mood and a syndrome, as well as a mental disorder. The mood is characterized by feelings of despondency, sadness and discouragement and is only one symptom of the mental disorder. When the mood persists, a syndrome of associated symptoms may arise, including diminished appetite, slowed thinking, a loss of interest in the world and feelings of guilt and hopelessness that are associated with a depressed mood.

The mental disorder (or disease) of depression is one of the most common psychiatric illnesses. It is classified as an *affective disorder,* or a disorder that alters an individual's expression of his or her *mood state.* Mood state refers to a prolonged emotion that affects one's entire emotional life. Depression is not merely sadness; it is a serious emotional disease that can render people unable to function, ruin their relationship with others and even lead to suicide.

Harry: A Case Study

Harry was 46 years old, happily married, and successfully employed as an accountant until his only daughter left home to go to college. For the first time in many years, Harry found himself all alone with his wife. He missed his daughter and began to have difficulty concentrating at work. He became increasingly irritable with his colleagues and his wife. Harry lost interest in food, stopped eating dinner and lost 12 pounds. Despite the fact that he was tired all the time, he could not sleep. He began to think he was a failure at his job, and fantasized about suicide.

It was obvious that Harry was sad. His face showed little expression and when he moved, it was in a painfully slow manner. No matter what his wife did to try to cheer him up, he felt as if he could never again find any pleasure in his life.

Harry had experienced a similar, though less severe, episode of depression at age 27. That episode, however, had lasted only three months before the pervasive feelings of sadness had completely disappeared.

The fact that Harry exhibited both mental and physical

Painful personal crises can trigger deep depressions, which can lead to thoughts of suicide. This is especially true for those who are psychologically or biochemically predisposed to this affliction. Psychiatrists are particularly inclined to prescibe antidepressant drugs to a patient who is potentially suicidal.

symptoms seemed to indicate that he was not merely unhappy that his daughter had left home, but that he was suffering from some sort of psychiatric disorder. Before he was diagnosed as depressed, however, the possibility of physical illness had to be ruled out. Cancer, thyroid imbalance and some neurological diseases produce symptoms similar to those characteristic of depression. Once the necessary tests had been evaluated, a psychiatrist was able to diagnose Harry's illness as depression. Depression is an especially dangerous illness because it often carries the risk of suicide. Harry had to be evaluated to determine whether he might commit suicide, and whether hospitalization might therefore be necessary. Whatever the decision, Harry's psychiatrist, in conjunction with Harry, also had to decide whether to treat him with antidepressant drugs and, if so, what kind.

The History of Treating Depression with Drugs

Prior to the 1950s, the anxiety and sleeplessness that often accompany depression could be treated only with sedatives, which took care of the symptoms but not the source of the disease. In 1957 the Swiss psychiatrist Roland Kuhn administered *imipramine* (a drug that resembles phenothiazine and

Art therapy is sometimes used to supplement drugs and psychotherapy in the treatment of mental illness. This elderly woman found that by making drawings of her inner "demons", she was able to dispel the terror they held for her.

which was originally created for its antihistamine and sedative properties) to various psychiatric patients. He noticed that although imipramine had no therapeutic effect on psychotic patients, depressed patients did respond positively to the drug after a few weeks of treatment.

In the years that followed, other scientists noticed that tuberculosis patients who were treated with the drug *iproniazid* also seemed to recover from depression. This observation led to the discovery of the group of antidepressants called *monoamine oxidase inhibitors* (see below).

The Chemical Basis of Depression

Soon after the development of antidepressant drugs, scientists developed a theory of how they worked. They already knew that reserpine (the antipsychotic and blood-pressure-lowering drug derived from the snakeroot plant of India) caused depression in some patients. Biochemical studies had shown that reserpine caused a release of amines (a type of chemical compound) in the brain that *decreased* the amount of neurotransmitters available for the transmission of information between the nerves.

Experiments on animals demonstrated that all of the drugs that had antidepressant properties *increased* the amount of amine neurotransmitters in the brain. Different antidepressants did this in different ways. The tricyclic antidepressants stopped the amines from being recycled, so that an excess of the neurotransmitters built up at the nerve endings. The monoamine oxidase inhibitors stopped the action of monoamine oxidase, which breaks down the amine transmitters, and thus also allowed a buildup of the neurotransmitters. From this information scientists hypothesized that depression was the result of a decrease in these amine transmitters in some part of the brain.

Since the hypothesis was formulated, additional data have shown this initial explanation of depression and the action of antidepressant drugs to be an oversimplification. Although in general the description is probably accurate, some drugs do not fit the theory, and there is still no adequate explanation of why all antidepressants take two weeks or more to produce their beneficial effects.

We need to remember that although depression is caused by chemical changes in the brain, these changes can be triggered by psychological factors. Sometimes, even when a person shows symptoms of the disease, we do not consider him or her clinically depressed (needing treatment). For example, people who suffer a great loss go through a period of mourning, frequently exhibiting all the symptoms of depression. However, mourning is considered a natural part of one's psychological life. Unlike true depression, it has a predictable course. Total recovery almost always occurs within several months without the use of drugs.

Drug Treatment

Two major groups of drugs are used to treat depression. The first group, which was mentioned previously, is the tricyclic

A painting by Robert Fleury shows French doctor Philippe Pinel unchaining mentally ill patients. Pinel was one of the first to think that insanity resulted from physiological causes rather than possession by demons.

antidepressants. The discussion of this group of drugs, however, will include some drugs that have different chemical structures but exhibit similar actions and side effects. The first tricyclic drug discovered, imipramine, can serve to illustrate this group of drugs.

Imipramine, like chlorpromazine, has *antihistaminic*

Maurits Cornelis Escher's 1951 lithograph House of Stairs *can be interpreted as a depiction of the sometimes bizarre, frenzied workings of the corporate world, an environment that has often been cited as a cause of acute anxiety and depression.*

effects, that is, it inhibits the action of histamine in the body, and thus reduces the allergic response (allergy pills and cold pills often include antihistamines). Imipramine also has atropine-like effects, which means that it causes dry mouth, widened pupils and urinary hesitancy. None of these actions seem to be necessary for imipramine's antidepressant effect.

A patient who takes imipramine, usually in the form of a pill or capsule, may first react by feeling sleepy. Although drowsiness is actually a side effect, it can be quite useful. Depression in any serious form is almost always accompanied by a disturbance in sleep. Some people cannot sleep at all, while others sleep too much. Imipramine will often remedy these problems in a day or so. A sleeping pill could also relieve the sleeplessness, but it would not treat the depression.

Imipramine and most other tricyclics prevent blood vessels from constricting normally, and can thus cause *postural hypotension* (decrease in blood pressure during a change in body position). Patients may experience dizziness when they stand up, the result of blood suddenly draining into the legs and causing a lack of blood in the brain. Patients are cautioned to stand up very slowly.

As mentioned earlier, one of the most serious problems in antidepressant treatment is that patients may suffer side effects almost immediately, without feeling the therapeutic benefits until they have taken the drug for several weeks. However, about a week after the therapeutic dose is reached, the depression lifts. The patients' images of themselves become more realistic, and their view of the world seems less bleak. They are able to concentrate, sleep better and feel "blue" less often. As their feelings of desperation and despair lessen, the idea of suicide fades.

Although the improvements come on slowly, in successful cases the patient's depression disappears within a month. Over three-quarters of patients suffering serious depressions can be helped significantly with the antidepressant drugs. Not all patients respond equally well to all the drugs. Doctors often need to test a patient's reactions to one or two different drugs before they can determine the most effective medicine for the patient.

Monoamine Oxidase Inhibitors

A patient who does not respond to the tricyclic antidepressants and similar drugs may try the *monoamine oxidase inhibitors.* Monoamine oxidase is an *enzyme* (an organic compound that induces chemical changes in other substances without being changed itself) that normally breaks down amines in the brain. When monoamine oxidase does not work properly, the amines accumulate in the brain. All the antidepressant drugs, including the drugs that inhibit the effect of the monoamine oxidase, produce a buildup of amines.

Although the monoamine oxidase inhibitors are often strikingly effective in treating depression, they can also cause serious side effects. Besides breaking down brain amines, monoamine oxidase has a number of other functions in the body. In the liver and intestines, monoamine oxidase breaks down some potentially toxic substances called amines which are formed by the fermentation of foodstuffs. Some, such as tyramine, have the potential to act as a drug on the heart and the blood vessels to increase blood pressure. Ordinarily, monoamine oxidase breaks up the tyramine before it can produce this effect. When monoamine oxidase is inhibited, however, the tyramine causes a release of naturally occurring amines. A serious, and even damaging, increase in blood pressure and subsequent stroke or heart attack can result.

When a person taking a monoamine oxidase inhibitor eats a tyramine-containing food, such as beer, wine, most cheeses and chicken liver, his or her blood pressure may rise suddenly. Doctors therefore stress that such patients must absolutely avoid the tyramine-containing foods. Because monoamine oxidase inhibitors also interact with some medicines, patients must check with their doctors before taking any other drugs.

Three monoamine oxidase inhibitors are used as antidepressants. They all have similar therapeutic effects and negative side effects. Phenelzine (Nardil), a representative of the group, may be prescribed for a depressed patient who does not respond to treatment with a tricyclic drug. Because the tricyclics and the monoamine oxidase inhibitors interact, the patient must wait at least a week between the last dose of tricyclic and the first treatment with phenelzine. Doctors must, of course, be careful to warn their patients about phenelzine's potentially dangerous interactions with foods and other drugs.

Patients taking phenelzine may experience dizziness, a result of the drug's blood-pressure-lowering effect. They may or may not get relief from whatever sleeping problems they are having. They may not notice the drug's full antidepressant effect for about two weeks, a delay which may be difficult for the patient. But, as with the tricyclics, after a period of time the drug's positive effects become apparent. The patient begins to enjoy life again, and experiences an improvement

AP/WIDE WORLD PHOTOS

The Pulitzer Prize-winning poet Anne Sexton holds her book Live or Die, *the title of which prophetically projected a challenge she faced during a series of depressions, culminating in her suicide in 1974.*

in his or her ability to concentrate. All the symptoms of the depression eventually disappear. Patients often continue to take these drugs for six months to a year, until the doctor is sure that the underlying disease has abated.

The monoamine oxidase inhibitors are usually the second choice of treatment and should be used only with patients who can be absolutely trusted to monitor their diet.

Other Treatments for Depression

Depression can also be treated with electroconvulsive shock therapy. Although it has gained a negative reputation, this form of therapy is the most consistently effective treatment for depression. Today, however, most psychiatrists reserve it for treating patients who do not respond to drugs.

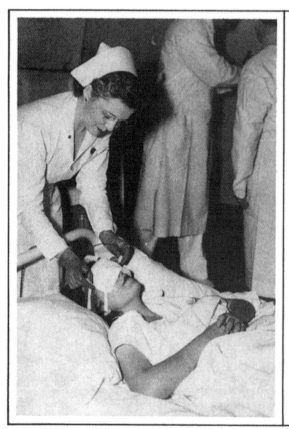

A nurse in a mental institution applies electric convulsive shock pads to the head of a psychotic patient. Although electric shock therapy has gained a negative reputation in recent years, it is an effective therapy for patients suffering from depression who do not respond to drugs.

AP/WIDE WORLD PHOTOS

Psychotherapy is a successful form of treatment for many mild depressions. Patients are more often treated with psychotherapy when the causes of the depression seem related to life crises, or to an inability to adjust or cope with the social environment. The use of antidepressant drugs is usually considered (1) if the depressed patient does not respond at all to psychotherapy within about ten visits; (2) if for over two weeks the patient has difficulty functioning and suffers from such physical symptoms as weight loss and serious sleep disturbance and (3) if a patient exhibits suicidal tendencies, in which case hospitalization should also be considered.

Extreme mood swings characterize manic depressives, people whose emotional states alternate between exaggerated feelings of well-being and severe depression. Anti-psychotic drugs are used to stabilize these moods and bring patients towards gradual recovery.

CHAPTER 4

MANIC-DEPRESSIVE PSYCHOSIS

One of the most serious psychiatric diseases is manic-depressive psychosis. Patients with this disease may have episodes of mania only, when they feel abnormally excited and have exaggerated feelings of well-being, or alternating episodes of mania and depression. In between these extreme mood swings, patients are often completely normal.

Andrew: A Case Study

Andrew, a 28-year-old, single computer programmer, came into his doctor's office looking very excited. Speaking quickly, jumping from topic to topic with great enthusiasm, he told the doctor that he had just written the most important computer programme ever developed. The doctor questioned him about his programme, whereupon Andrew became very irritable and suspicious. As he paced about the office, he explained that the Japanese had been trying to steal his secrets. He had even telephoned various people in Japan to question them about their involvement in computer theft, and his phone bills were five times higher than normal. In the middle of his story he suddenly started to cry, but just as quickly he cheered up again and described the new company he was planning to establish with money from friends. He told the doctor he had been giving elaborate gifts to everyone he knew, "to reward them for their support".

Andrew's expansive mood, his irritability, and his quick mood shifts are all typical of what psychiatrists call "mania". Patients who suffer from this illness may not be happy or euphoric, but their mood state is always expansive. They sleep very little and can even die from exhaustion. They frequently squander money and alienate friends. Severe paranoia and aggressiveness are common.

The History of Treating Manic-Depressives

Before the development of effective drug treatment, manic patients were more difficult to control than any other group among the mentally ill. They rode a dangerous roller coaster through life, sometimes swinging rapidly from the heights of mania to the extreme depths of depression. Before 1950, ineffective sleep therapies and shock treatments were the only methods available for the treatment of mania.

In 1949 Dr John Cade began to study the basis of mania. Thinking that some toxin secreted by the body might induce the manic state, he compared the urine of manic patients to

A Vietnamese refugee is interviewed by a psychiatrist, as a nurse and an interpreter look on. Before any course of treatment for manic-depressive patients is prescribed, the treating doctor must make an accurate diagnosis. In many cases, this will involve special tests such as brain scans and blood tests, in addition to extensive interviews. Details about a patient's background often provides clues on how to treat present problems.

UPI/BETTMANN NEWSPHOTOS

that of other patients. In laboratory experiments with guinea pigs, he discovered that the urine from manic patients was, in fact, more toxic than other urine. The toxic substance appeared to be a *urate,* a chemical normally found in urine, but in smaller quantities.

Cade already knew that lithium binds, or combines, with urates to produce lithium urate, a compound that will readily dissolve in water. Therefore, he hypothesized, administering lithium to the animals might protect them from the toxic effects of the urates. In fact, he discovered that not only did lithium protect the animals, but it also seemed to sedate them. His next step was to try the lithium on manic patients. Within a few days of administering the drug, Cade noted that the mania abated, and over the course of a few weeks, it entirely disappeared.

Although further research showed that Cade was wrong

Finding healthy ways to deal with anger is often one of the keys to mental health. Although manic-depressive illness has not been specifically linked to environmental factors, it is known that if it is not properly vented, unreasonable anger in children can lead to a lifetime of problematic emotional duress.

about *how* lithium worked, he had discovered an effective substance to treat mania. Cade's success was reported in a paper published in the *Medical Journal of Australia,* but unlike the medical profession's immediate positive response to chlorpromazine, this report was received unenthusiastically. Not until 20 years later was the discovery of lithium recognized. Today, lithium is an accepted medicine for the prevention of recurrent manic episodes, for the treatment of acute mania, and for the treatment of depression in manic-depressive patients.

The Psychopharmacology of Lithium

Lithium is a chemical element that occurs in nature as a white metal. In medicine, lithium is used in the form of a carbonate salt (combined with the compound H_2CO_3). Therefore, the term lithium actually refers to lithium carbonate. Though rather simple in structure, lithium has very complex actions in the body. The exact basis for these actions is still unknown.

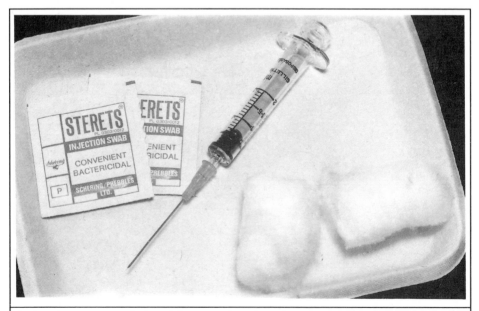

Drugs that are metabolized (broken down) by the liver can alternatively be injected. This facilitates greater strength reaching the brain, before any metabolism occurs.

Although lithium is not normally found in the body, it resembles both sodium and potassium, chemicals that are necessary for the functioning of all the body's nerves. To some degree, lithium is able to substitute for sodium and potassium.

Lithium increases an individual's white blood cell count, and therefore is sometimes used to help people who have low "white counts" owing to cancer-treatment drugs. And finally, the drug affects the functioning of the brain, perhaps because of its ability to alter the brain's amine balance.

Like other psychotherapeutic drugs, lithium takes some time to produce its therapeutic effect. When patients first begin taking the drug they may experience fine tremors of the hands and an increase in both thirst and urination. Lithium may also affect the thyroid gland (a gland located in the neck that produces a hormone that affects growth, development, and metabolic rate). It can cause a reversible goitre (an enlargement of the thyroid gland that produces symptoms such as bulging eyeballs, tremors of the fingers and

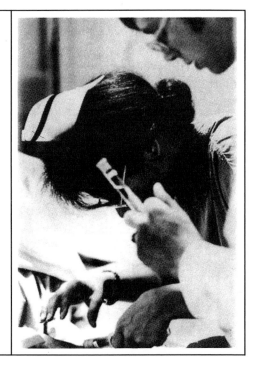

Blood is drawn to test for levels of lithium, a salt-like mineral used to control—and prevent—maniacal episodes. In 1949 the Australian psychiatrist John Cade discovered that lithium could be used to treat mania, but it took 20 years before the importance of his discovery was fully recognized.

hands and an increase in metabolic rate) or *hypothyroidism* (a decrease in thyroid secretions that causes a lowered metabolic rate and such symptoms as obesity, low blood pressure and pulse and depressed muscular activity). Because lithium is often used to *prevent* illness, doctors must keep in mind that in healthy individuals lithium produces tremors and increased urination, and can have a slight sedating effect, which is rarely considered unpleasant.

In manic patients, lithium is considered a mood-stabilizing drug. It slowly decreases irritability, aggressiveness and the rapid flowing of ideas, and reduces the patient's expansive mood. It also decreases paranoia and, if hallucinations are present, they disappear. Lithium can have remarkable effects on anger and aggressiveness, and on such recurring diseases as *periodic catatonia,* a rare syndrome of repeated episodes of rigidity and loss of speech. Although lithium acts like an antipsychotic drug in its effect on mania, it has no effect on most other psychoses. This seems to indicate a common chemical basis for a whole pattern of symptoms. Despite this tantalizing lead, scientists are still mystified as to what is the chemical basis of manic-depressive psychosis.

Lithium is quickly absorbed from the stomach and distributed throughout the body. Patients must therefore almost always take the drug in several doses during the day. (It thus differs from the antidepressant and antipsychotic drugs, which can be taken in one daily dose at bedtime.) Because only a narrow margin exists between the therapeutic dose of lithium and the amount that can bring on toxic symptoms, patients taking lithium regularly undergo blood tests to monitor the level of the drug in their blood. These tests also help doctors determine whether the drug is being taken properly and whether the dosage is correct.

As the sodium level in the body decreases, the lithium level increases. When the lithium level gets too high, a patient may become confused and suffer from nausea and diarrhoea. In order to avoid these symptoms, patients who take lithium and do strenuous physical work or exercise should supplement their diet with salt pills. They should always avoid low-sodium diets.

Manic-depressive psychosis very often cannot be cured,

and many patients continue to be treated with lithium all their lives. In the past some doctors believed that long-term lithium treatment could damage the kidneys. However, current opinion is that as long as the patient's urine is analyzed periodically, lithium may be taken on a long-term basis. As discussed earlier, lithium can also adversely affect the thyroid gland, and patients on lithium must be tested regularly to ensure that the thyroid is functioning properly.

Because not all patients respond positively to lithium treatments, and a few cannot tolerate the side effects, a number of new drugs are being studied. The most promising of these is *carbamazepine* (Tegretol), a drug used in the treatment of epilepsy. Carbamazepine in many ways resembles lithium in its pharmacologic action. It has been found effective in treating mania and in preventing recurrent manic illness. However, because of the serious side effects sometimes produced by this drug (blood-cell abnormalities, heart failure, dizziness, blurred vision, fever and vomiting), carbamazepine is used as a second choice, after the safer drugs have proven to be ineffective or inappropriate.

People who take lithium and exercise strenuously should supplement their diets with salt pills. This is because the loss of sodium that heavy perspiration causes, coupled with rising levels of lithium in the body, can lead to some serious and unpleasant side effects.

A psychiatrist examines the results of a sleep survey, which will enable him to predict which one of several available antidepressant drugs will be the most effective for his patient.

CHAPTER 5

THE FUTURE

Until recently, drugs that have proved effective in treating mental illness were discovered by scientists and doctors whose research and clinical experience altered them to the psychiatric potential of a particular substance. By modifying the molecular structure of the original chemical they were then able to develop additional drugs. Because we do not have any adequate animal models of mental illness, we have been restricted in the development of new drugs.

The discovery of psychotherapeutic drugs has led to research into the amine systems of the brain, which, in turn, has provided more information about the chemistry of the brain. Newer techniques, such as PET scanning (a method by which radioactive isotopes are used to visualize the brain's chemistry) and Magnetic Resonance Imaging (a technique that uses giant magnets to create images of the anatomy of the brain and determine its chemistry), give us hope that in the future we will be able to visualize how mental illness alters the brain's chemistry. With this information, researchers will be able to design new drugs to correct abnormal chemical states and thus effectively treat mental disease.

Even though we know that mental illness has a chemical basis, we must not ignore the psychological dimensions of the disease. Drugs can be only one aspect of the treatment programme for mental illness. Mental health professionals must also pay close attention to the complex needs and emotions of every patient in order to help that individual achieve a stronger sense of self and a healthier means of relating to his or her environment.

APPENDIX 1

SYMPTOMS OF CLINICAL DEPRESSION

A. Dysphoric mood, which is characterized by a loss of interest or pleasure in all or almost all usual activities and pastimes. Someone suffering from dysphoric mood might say that he or she feels depressed, sad, blue, hopeless, low, or down in the dumps. The mood disturbance must be prominent and relatively persistent, but not necessarily the most dominant symptom, and it does not include momentary shifts from one dysphoric mood to another dysphoric mood (e.g., anxiety to depression to anger), such as are seen in states of acute psychotic turmoil.

B. At least four of the following symptoms will each be present nearly every day for a period of at least two weeks:

> 1. Poor appetite or significant weight loss (even though the person is not dieting) *or* increased appetite or significant weight gain
> 2. Insomnia or, conversely, hypersomnia (sleeping for extreme periods of time)
> 3. Psychomotor agitation or retardation (not merely subjectiveness feelings of restlessness or being "slowed down")
> 4. Loss of interest or pleasure in usual activities; decrease in sexual drive
> 5. Loss of energy; fatigue
> 6. Feelings of worthlessness, self-reproach, or excessive or inappropriate guilt
> 7. Complaints or evidence of diminished ability to think or concentrate
> 8. Recurrent thoughts of death and suicide, a desire to be dead, or an attempt at suicide

APPENDIX 2

SYMPTOMS OF MANIA

A. One or more distinct periods with a predominantly elevated, expansive, or irritable mood. The elevated or irritable mood must be a prominent part of the illness and relatively persistent, although it may alternate or intermingle with depressive mood.

B. Duration of at least one week during which at least three of the following symptoms persist and are present to a significant degree:

1. Increase in activity (either socially, at work, or sexually) or physical restlessness
2. Increased talkativeness
3. A subjective experience that thoughts are racing
4. Inflated self-esteem (grandiosity, which may be delusional)
5. Decreased need for sleep
6. Distractibility (i.e., attention too easily drawn to unimportant or irrelevant external stimuli)
7. Excessive involvement in activities that have a high potential for painful consequences, a risk which is not recognized by the person; activities can include buying sprees, sexual indiscretions, foolish business investments and reckless driving

APPENDIX 3

SYMPTOMS OF SCHIZOPHRENIA

A. At least one of the following during a phase of the illness:

    1. Bizarre delusions (content is patently absurd and has *no* possible basis in fact, such as delusions of being controlled, thought broadcasting, thought insertion, or thought withdrawal)

    2. Grandiose, religious, nihilistic, or other delusions

    3. Delusions with persecutory or jealous content, if accompanied by hallucinations of any type

    4. Auditory hallucinations in which either a voice keeps up a running commentary of the individual's behaviour or thoughts, or two or more voices converse with each other

    5. Auditory hallucinations on several occasions with content having no apparent relation to depression or elation

    6. Incoherence, marked loosening of associations, markedly illogical thinking, or marked poverty of content of speech if associated with at least one of the following:

  a. Apathy, or lack of involvement with the world

  b. Delusions or hallucinations

  c. Catatonic or other grossly disorganized behaviour

B. Deterioration from a previous level of functioning in such areas as work, social relations, and self-care.

C. Duration: continuous signs of the illness for at least six months at some time during the person's life, with some signs of the illness at present.

D. At least two of the following symptoms:

    1. Social isolation or withdrawal

    2. Marked impairment in role functioning as wage earner, student, and/or homeworker

    3. Markedly peculiar behaviour (e.g., collecting

rubbish, talking to self in public, hoarding food)
4. Marked impairment in personal hygiene and grooming
5. Apathetic appearance
6. Digressive, vague, overelaborate, circumstantial, or
   metaphorical speech
7. Odd or bizarre thought processes (e.g., supersti-
   tiousness, or fantasies of clairvoyance or tele-
   pathy)
8. Unusual perceptual experiences (e.g., recurrent
   illusions, sensing the presence of a force or
   person not actually present)

Some Useful Addresses

Agencies involved in the prevention and treatment of mental illness

In the United Kingdom:

Manic Depression Fellowship
51 Sheen Road, Richmond, Surrey TW9 1YG

Mental Health Foundation
8 Hallam Street, London W1N 6DY

MIND
22 Harley Street, London W1N 2ED

National Schizophrenia Fellowship
78 Victoria Road, Surbiton, Surrey KT6 4NS

In Australia:

Association of Relatives and Friends of the Mentally Ill
311 Hay Street, Subiaco, Western Australia 6008

Australian National Association for Mental Health
1 Cookson Street, Campberwell, Victoria, Australia 3124

In New Zealand:

The Foundation
PO Box 5367, Wellesley, Auckland

Mental Health Foundation of New Zealand
PO Box 37483, Parnell, Auckland

In South Africa:

South African National Council for Mental Health
PO Box 2587, Johannesburg, SA 2000

Further Reading

DSM-IIIR, 3rd edition. Washington, DC: American Psychiatric Association, 20, 1980.

Duquesne, T. *Essential Drugs: a Consumer Formulary.* London: Heterdox, 1987.

Gillies, D. and Lader, M. *Guide to the Use of Psychotropic Drugs.* Edinburgh: Churchill Livingstone, 1986.

Gilman, A.G., Goodman, L.S., Rall, T.W. and Murad, F. *The Pharmacological Basis of Therapeutics,* 7th edition. New York: Macmillan Publishing Co. Inc., 1985.

Swazey, J.P. *Chlorpromazine in Psychiatry: A Study of Therapeutic Innovation.* Cambridge, Massachusetts: MIT Press, 1974.

Glossary

addiction a condition caused by repeated drug use, characterized by a compulsive urge to continue using the drug, a tendency to increase the dosage, and physiological and/or psychological dependence

affective disorder a disorder that alters the expression of an individual's mood state

akathisia a condition sometimes produced by antipsychotic drugs and characterized by restlessness and an inability to sit down because the thought of doing so produces extreme anxiety

anaesthetic a drug that produces loss of sensation, sometimes with loss of consciousness

antidepressant drug a drug that acts to relieve the symptoms of depression

antihistamine a drug that inhibits the action of histamine and thus reduces the allergic response

antipsychotic drug a drug, such as chlorpromazine, that calms a person who is in a psychotic state

axon the part of the neuron along which the nerve impulse travels away from the cell body

barbiturate a drug that causes depression of the central nervous system; generally used to reduce anxiety

benzodiazepine antianxiety and sedative drugs such as Valium

chlorpromazine a tranquillizing drug, used in the treatment of psychotic states

cocaine the primary psychoactive ingredient in the coca plant; used as a behavioural stimulant

delusion a false belief that is not based on external stimulation and that is inconsistent with the individual's knowledge and personal experiences

dendrite the hairlike structure that protrudes from and carries signals towards the neural cell body, and on which receptor sites are located

depression a sometimes overwhelming emotional state characterized by feelings of inadequacy and hopelessness, accompanied by a decrease in physical and psychological activity

dopamine a neurotransmitter produced by the adrenal gland; it has a marked effect on body temperature and metabolic rate and on the nervous system and cardiovascular system

dopamine-blocking drug a drug that interferes with the transmission of nerve impulses in the body by blocking the action of dopamine in the body

electroshock therapy a technique sometimes effective in treating agitated psychosis, characterized by the use of an electric current to stimulate the brain and induce involuntary muscle contractions

enzyme an organic compound that induces chemical changes in other substances without being changed itself

galactorrhea the extreme flow of milk from the female breast, sometimes caused by chlorpromazine

goitre an enlargement of the thyroid gland, producing symptoms such as bulging eyeballs, tremors of the fingers and hands, and an increase in metabolic rate

hallucination a sensory impression that has no basis in reality

hashish a psychoactive substance made from the resin and the dried and pressed flowers and leaves of the marijuana plant

hypnotic a drug that induces sleep or dulls the senses

hypotension a decrease in blood pressure

hypothyroidism a decrease in thyroid secretion that causes a lowered metabolic rate, and such symptoms as obesity, low blood pressure and pulse, and depressed muscular activity

lithium a chemical element that occurs in nature as a white metal and is used to prevent recurrent manic episodes and to treat manic-depressive psychosis

lobotomy a type of brain surgery that severs communication between specific parts of the brain and is sometimes used to relieve some forms of mental illness

LSD lysergic acid diethylamide; a hallucinogen derived from a fungus that grows on rye or from morning-glory seeds

manic characterized by excitement and mental and physical hyperactivity

manic-depressive psychosis a mental disorder characterized by abrupt alternations of depression and mania

metabolism the chemical changes in the living cell by which energy is provided for the vital processes and activities and by which new material is assimilated to repair cell structures; or, the process that uses enzymes to convert one substance into compounds that can be easily eliminated from the body

mood-stabilizing drug a drug that reduces or eliminates fluctuations in mood

mood state a prolonged emotion that affects one's entire emotional life

neuroleptic a drug that produces symptoms that resemble the symptoms of diseases of the nervous system

neuron a cell that conducts electrochemical signals

neurotic related to a disorder of the thought processes that is not characterized by a loss of contact with reality and not due to a disease of the nervous system; symptoms include fatigue, anxiety, compulsiveness, and hypochondria

neurotransmitter a chemical that travels from the axon of one neuron, across the synaptic gap, and to the receptor site on the dendrite of an adjacent neuron, thus allowing communication between neural cells

organic brain syndrome a large group of mental disorders resulting from brain damage due to physical illness or trauma

paranoia a mental condition characterized by suspiciousness, fear, delusions, and, in extreme cases, hallucinations

parasympathetic nervous system the part of the central nervous system that controls involuntary bodily activity such as sweating and contraction of the intestine

Parkinson's disease a chronic nervous disease that creates a lack of dopamine in certain brain cells; it produces symptoms such as fine tremors, facial expressionlessness, and muscle weakness and rigidity; its cause is unknown, though it mainly affects older people

PCP phencyclidine; a drug first used as an anaesthetic but later discontinued because of its severe adverse side effects; today abused for its stimulant, depressant, and/or hallucinogenic effects

periodic catatonia   a rare syndrome of repeated episodes of rigidity and loss of speech

phenothiazine   the parent chemical from which a certain class of tranquillizers that include chlorpromazine is synthesized

placebo effect   a pharmacologic effect on a symptom produced by a substance that is either pharmacologically inert (produces no effects on the body) or is active only in the treatment of unrelated symptoms

prolactin   a hormone that stimulates milk production in nursing mothers

psychiatrist   a medical doctor who has continued his or her education to study mental disease and who is trained to distinguish between the symptoms of physical disease or neurological illness and psychological disease; he or she can prescribe drugs

psychoanalysis   a form of psychotherapy that grew out of Austrian neurologist Sigmund Freud's (1856-1939) observations of neurotics; based on the theory that mental illness is caused by the repression of painful or undesirable past experiences and that by bringing forgotten memories to the surface, the source of psychological conflicts can be located; proponents believe that the patient's awareness of the conflicts reduces or eliminates psychological disorders

psychologist   a person who usually has an advanced degree, often an Ph.D., in clinical psychology and who practices one or more of the many types of psychotherapy

psychopharmacology   the study of the effects of drugs on the mind

psychosis   abnormal or pathological behaviour that includes the loss of touch with reality, and occasionally hallucinations and delusions

psychosurgery   surgical intervention into the brain to treat neurological disorders

psychotherapeutic   a drug that is used in the treatment of psychological disorders

psychotherapist   an individual trained to use one of the many forms of therapy that evolved from the study of human behaviour and the psychological theories that developed; psychotherapists treat disorders not with drugs but through techniques such as suggestions, reeducation, hypnotism, and psychoanalysis

reserpine   a drug with tranquillizing effects that is extracted from the root of *Rauwolfia serpentina,* a plant native to India, and used in the treatment of psychosis

schizophrenia a chronic disorder characterized by a loss of touch with reality and symptoms such as paranoia, delusions, and hallucinations

sedative   a drug that produces a soothing or tranquillizing effect

sympathetic nervous system   a system of nerves within the central nervous system that, during an emergency, elicits responses of alertness, excitement, and alarm and controls the expenditure of necessary energy

synaptic gap   the gap between the axon and dendrite of two adjacent neurons across which neurotransmitters travel

tardive dyskinesia   a neurological effect of antipsychotic-drug use that occurs late in treatment and is characterized by involuntary mouth movements, and in severe cases, slow, rhythmic, automatic arm and torso movements

thyroid gland   a gland located in the neck that produces a hormone that effects growth, development, and metabolic rate

tolerance   a decrease of susceptibility to the effects of a drug due to its continued administration, resulting in the user's need to increase the drug dosage in order to achieve the effects experienced previously

tranquillizer   a drug that has calming, relaxing effects

tricyclic antidepressants   a class of drugs whose members have three rings of carbon atoms in each molecule, and that is used therapeutically to relieve depression and elevate mood in individuals who are psychologically depressed

urate   a chemical normally found in the urine

Index

Robert Byck, M.D., is a professor of psychiatry and pharmacology at Yale University School of Medicine and a practicing clinical psychiatrist and pharmacologist. He was the editor of Freud's *Cocaine Papers*.

Solomon H. Snyder, M.D., is Distinguished Service Professor of Neuroscience, Pharmacology and Psychiatry at The Johns Hopkins University School of Medicine. He has served as president of the Society for Neuroscience and in 1978 received the Albert Laster Award in Medical Research. He is the author of *Uses of Marijuana, Madness and the Brain, The Troubled Mind, Biological Aspects of Mental Disorder,* and has edited *Perspective in Neuropharmacology: A Tribute to Julius Axelrod.* Professor Snyder was a research associate with Dr Axelrod at the National Institute of Health.

Malcolm Lader, D.Sc., Ph.D.,M.D., F.R.C. Psych. is Professor of Clinical Psychopharmacology at the Institute of Psychiatry, University of London and Honorary Consultant to the Bethlam Royal and Maudsley Hospitals. He is a member of the External Scientific Staff of the Medical Research Council. He has researched extensively into the actions of drugs used to treat psychiatric illness and symptoms, in particular the tranquillizers. He has written several books and over 300 scientific articles. Professor Lader is a member of several governmental advisory committees concerned with drugs.